NO MORE!

A Gallery of Protests and Demonstrations

Photographs and Posters
from the Library of Congress

Pomegranate
SAN FRANCISCO

Pomegranate Communications, Inc.
Box 808022, Petaluma CA 94975
800 227 1428; www.pomegranate.com

Pomegranate Europe Ltd.
Unit 1, Heathcote Business Centre, Hurlbutt Road
Warwick, Warwickshire CV34 6TD, UK
[+44] 0 1926 430111; sales@pomeurope.co.uk

ISBN 978-0-7649-4589-2
Pomegranate Catalog No. AA441

Compiled and edited by Athena Angelos

Pomegranate publishes books of postcards on a wide range of subjects.
Please contact the publisher for more information.

Cover designed by Shannon Lemme
Printed in Korea
17 16 15 14 13 12 11 10 09 08 10 9 8 7 6 5 4 3 2 1

To facilitate detachment of the postcards from this book, fold each card along its perforation line before tearing.

From the Boston Tea Party to the Declaration of Independence to the civil rights movement of the 1950s and 1960s, protest against perceived injustices has been as much a part of the American experience as baseball and jazz. The Bill of Rights amending the US Constitution guarantees free speech and assembly (meeting together), protecting the right of the rabble to rouse. "The spirit of resistance to government is so valuable on certain occasions, that I wish it to be always kept alive," stated Thomas Jefferson, who also added, "The will of the people is the only legitimate foundation of any government, and to protect its free expression should be our first object." The poet Ella Wheeler Wilcox wrote, "To sin by silence when they should protest / Makes cowards of men."

Throughout their country's history, Americans have found many occasions not to keep silent "when they should protest." This set of thirty images from the collections of the Library of Congress shows them rejecting the tyranny of Britain's King George III as they tear down his statue in 1776; crusading for the abolition of slavery; speaking out against unfair working conditions for children, women, and all laborers; calling for temperance and women's suffrage; demanding that civil liberties be maintained in wartime; demonstrating for civil rights and against the war in Vietnam; and supporting prisoners' rights while rejecting capital punishment. In the twenty-first century, artists silently plea for a peaceful US response to the terrorist attacks of September 11, 2001.

A protest may not be popular with everyone, but in the United States, where each person is entitled to express an opinion, the other side has the right to disagree and protest too. This dialogue is essential in a country founded by the people, of the people, and for the people. Dissent is not disloyalty but a responsibility. It is how informed citizens ensure a government that is open, responsive, and just. Silence and apathy, conversely, threaten our freedoms. It is, as has been said, "the glorious noise of democracy," raised in discussion, debate, and reform, that keeps us on our toes.

n southport chicago illinois 60657
SI·SE·PUEDE~IT·CAN·BE·DONE
BOYCOTT LETTUCE & GRAPES

NO MORE! A Gallery of Protests and Demonstrations

Si Se Puede—It Can Be Done poster encouraging the boycott of lettuce and grapes to protest the unfair treatment of migrant laborers, Chicago Women's Graphics Collective, 1978. Yanker Poster Collection, Prints and Photographs Division, LC-USZC4-2420

707 782 9000   WWW.POMEGRANATE.COM

ABOLISH
SLAVERY

NO MORE! A Gallery of Protests and Demonstrations

Girls at a labor parade wearing banners printed in English and Yiddish, New York City, 1909. News service photograph. George Grantham Bain Collection, Prints and Photographs Division, LC-DIG-ppmsca-06591

707 782 9000 WWW.POMEGRANATE.COM

A
RESTAURANT
CAFÉ

NO MORE! A Gallery of Protests and Demonstrations

Newly unionized stage actors gather on 45th Street in New York City during the strike of 1919, which shut down more than 50 shows for 30 days. News service photograph. George Grantham Bain Collection, Prints and Photographs Division, LC-B2-4997-10

707 782 9000 WWW.POMEGRANATE.COM

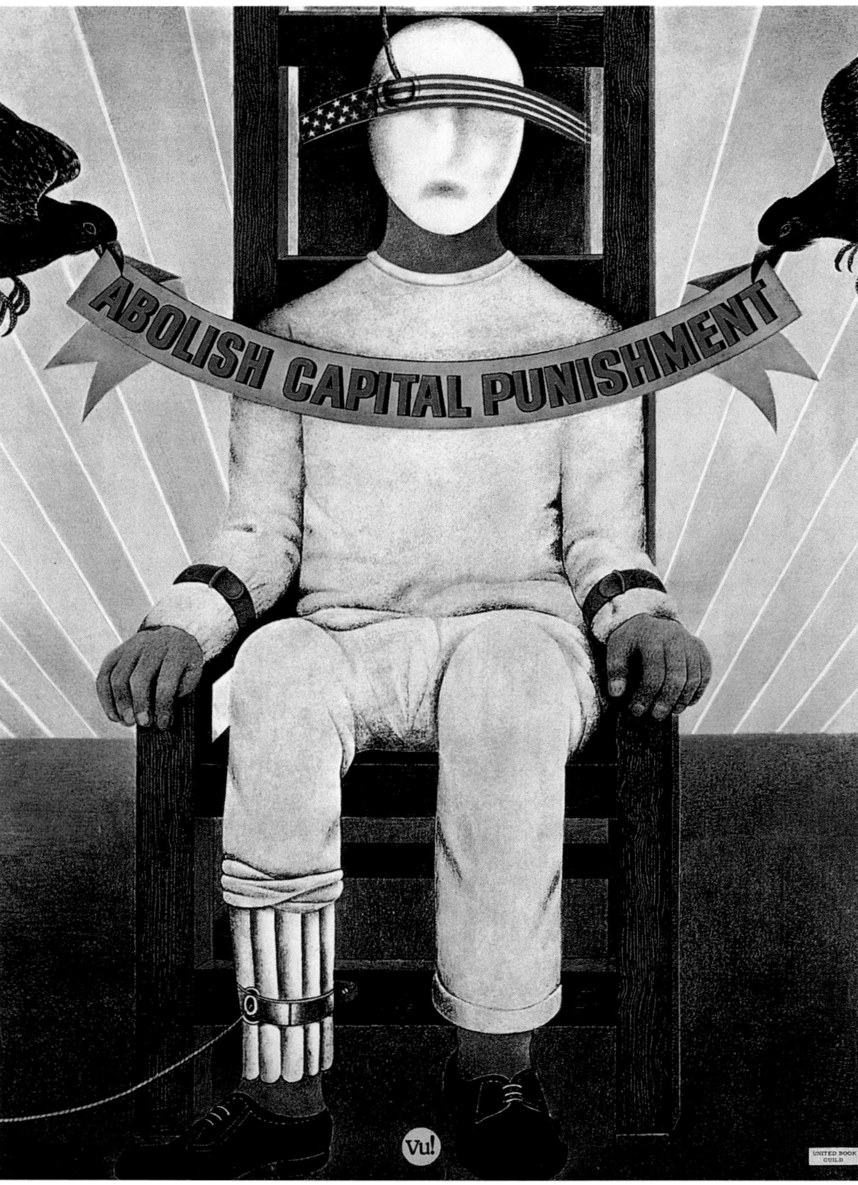
ABOLISH CAPITAL PUNISHMENT
Vu!
UNITED BOOK GUILD

NO MORE! **A Gallery of Protests and Demonstrations**

Abolish Capital Punishment poster by Vu! and United Book Guild, c. 1967. Yanker Poster Collection, Prints and Photographs Division, LC-USZC4-2883

707 782 9000 WWW.POMEGRANATE.COM

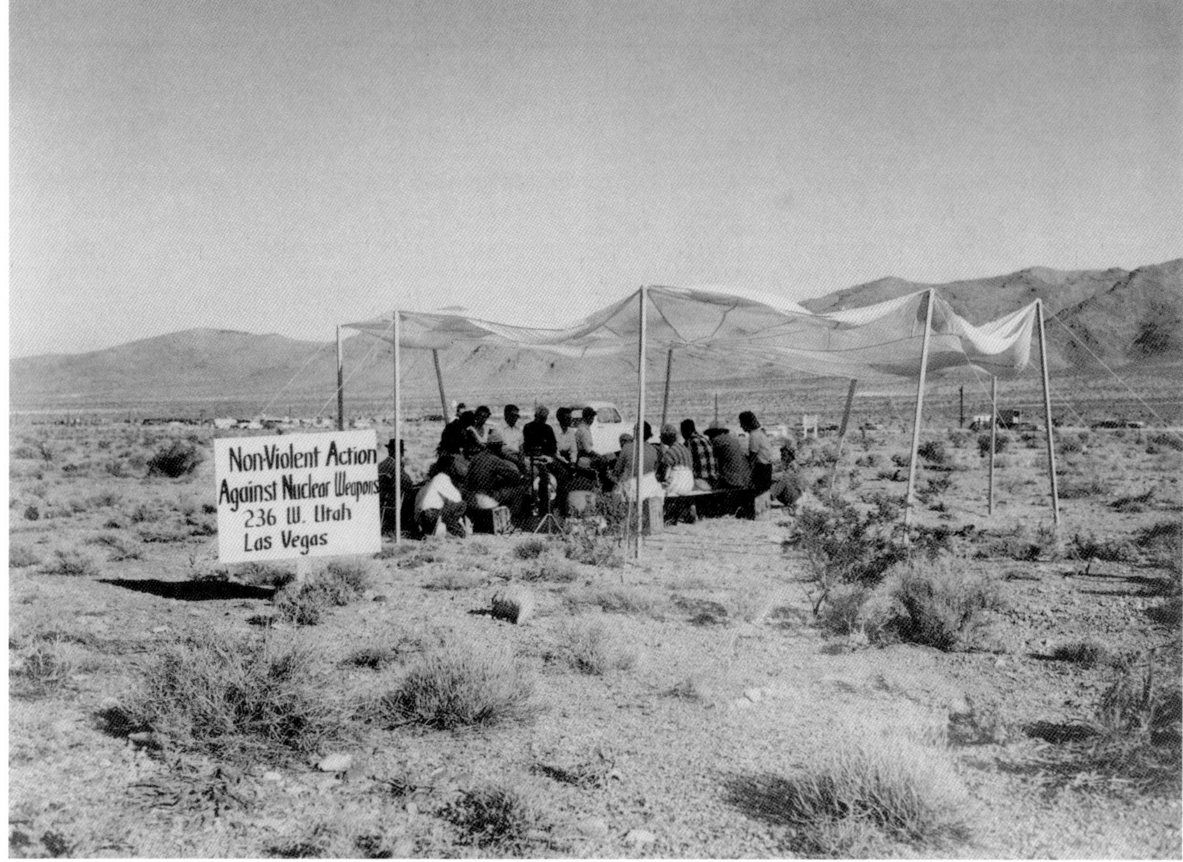
Non-Violent Action
Against Nuclear Weapons
236 W. Utah
Las Vegas

NO MORE! A Gallery of Protests and Demonstrations

Members of Non-violent Action Against Nuclear Weapons in prayer vigil prior to attempted entry into a Nevada nuclear test site, August 6, 1957. Photograph, gift of *Encyclopedia Britannica*. Prints and Photographs Division, LC-USZ62-123101

707 782 9000 WWW.POMEGRANATE.COM

AM I NOT A MAN AND A BROTHER?

OUR COUNTRYMEN IN CHAINS!

By J. G. WHITTIER.

"The despotism which our fathers could not bear in their native country is expiring, and the sword of justice in her reformed hands has applied its exterminating edge to slavery. Shall the United States—the Free United States, which could not bear the bonds of a king, cradle the bondage which a king is abolishing? Shall a Republic be less free than a Monarchy? Shall we, in the vigor and buoyancy of our manhood, be less energetic in righteousness, than a kingdom in its age?—*Dr. Follen's Address.*

Genius of America! Spirit of our free institutions—where art thou? How art thou fallen, oh Lucifer! son of the morning—how art thou fallen from Heaven! Hell from beneath is moved for thee, to meet thee at thy coming!—The kings of the earth cry out to thee, Aha! Aha!—ART THOU BECOME LIKE UNTO US?—*Speech of Rev. S. J. May.*

OUR FELLOW COUNTRYMEN IN CHAINS!
  SLAVES—in a land of light and law!—
SLAVES—crouching on the very plains
  Where rolled the storm of Freedom's war!
A groan from Eutaw's haunted wood—
  A wail where Camden's martyrs fell—
By every shrine of patriot blood,
  From Moultrie's wall and Jasper's well!

By storied hill and hallowed grot,
  By mossy wood and marshy glen,
Whence rang of old the rifle shot,
  And hurrying shout of Marion's men!—
The groan of breaking hearts is there—
  The falling lash—the fetter's clank!—
Slaves—SLAVES are breathing in that air
  Which old De Kalb and Sumpter drank!

What, ho!—*our* countrymen in chains!—
  The whip on WOMAN'S shrinking flesh!
Our soil yet reddening with the stains,
  Caught from her scourging, warm and fresh!
What! mothers from their children riven!—
  What! God's own image bought and sold!—
AMERICANS to market driven,
  And bartered as the brute for *gold*!

Speak!—shall their agony of prayer
  Come thrilling to our hearts in vain!
To us—whose fathers scorned to bear
  The paltry *menace* of a chain;—
To us whose boast is loud and long
  Of holy liberty and light—
Say, shall these writhing slaves of Wrong
  Plead vainly for their plundered Right?

What!—shall we send, with lavish breath,
  Our sympathies across the wave,
Where manhood on the field of death
  Strikes for his freedom, or a grave!—
Shall prayers go up—and hymns be sung
  For Greece, the Moslem fetter spurning—
And millions hail with pen and tongue
  Our light on all her altars burning!

Shall Belgium feel, and gallant France,
  By Vendome's pile and Schoenbrun's wall,
And Poland, gasping on her lance,
  The impulse of our cheering call?
And shall the SLAVE, beneath our eye,
  Clank o'er *our* fields his hateful chain?
And toss his fettered arm on high,
  And groan for freedom's gift, in vain?

Oh say, shall Prussia's banner be
  A refuge for the stricken slave;—
And shall the Russian serf go free
  By Baikal's lake and Neva's wave;—
And shall the wintry-bosomed Dane
  Relax the iron hand of pride,
And bid his bondmen cast the chain
  From fettered soul and limb, aside?

Shall every flap of England's flag*
  Proclaim that all around are free,
From 'farthest Ind' to each blue crag
  That beetles o'er the Western Sea?
And shall we scoff at Europe's kings,
  When Freedom's fire is dim with us,
And round our country's altar clings
  The damning shade of Slavery's curse?

Go—let us ask of Constantine
  To loose his grasp on Poland's throat—
And beg the lord of Mahmoud's line
  To spare the struggling Suliote.
Will not the scorching answer come
  From turbaned Turk, and fiery Russ—
'Go, loose your fettered slaves at home,
  Then turn and ask the like of us!'

Just God! and shall we calmly rest,
  The christian's scorn—the heathen's mirth—
Content to live the lingering jest
  And by-word of a mocking earth?
Shall our own glorious land retain
  That curse which Europe scorns to bear?
Shall our own brethren drag the chain
  Which not even Russia's menials wear?

Up, then, in Freedom's manly part,
  From gray-beard eld to fiery youth,
And on the nation's naked heart
  Scatter the living coals of Truth.
Up—while ye slumber, deeper yet
  The shadow of our fame is growing—
Up—While ye pause, our sun may set
  In blood, around our altars flowing!

Oh rouse ye—ere the storm comes forth—
  The gathered wrath of God and man—
Like that which wasted Egypt's earth,
  When hail and fire above it ran.
Hear ye no warnings in the air?
  Feel ye no earthquake underneath?
Up—up—why will ye slumber where
  The sleeper only wakes in death?

Up now for Freedom!—not in strife
  Like that your sterner fathers saw
The awful waste of human life—
  The glory and the guilt of war:
But break the chain—the yoke remove
  And smite to earth oppression's rod,
With those mild arms of Truth and Love,
  Made mighty through the living God!

Prone let the shrine of Moloch sink,
  And leave no traces where it stood
Nor longer let its idol drink
  His daily cup of human blood:
But rear another altar there,
  To truth and love and mercy given,
And Freedom's gift and Freedom's prayer
  Shall call an answer down from Heaven!

He that stealeth a man and selleth him, or if he be found in his hand, he shall surely be put to death. Exod. xxi. 16.

* ENGLAND has 800,000 Slaves, and she has made them FREE. America has 2,250,000!—and she HOLDS THEM FAST!!!

Sold at the Anti-Slavery Office, 144 Nassau Street. Price TWO CENTS Single; or $1.00 per hundred.

NO MORE! A Gallery of Protests and Demonstrations

Am I Not a Man and a Brother? This design was originally used as the seal of the Society for the Abolition of Slavery in England in the 1780s. Woodcut on wove paper, American Anti-Slavery Society, 1837. Prints and Photographs Division, LC-USZC4-5321

707 782 9000 WWW.POMEGRANATE.COM

Bill of Rights

Congress OF THE United States,

begun and held at the City of New York, on Wednesday, the fourth of March, one thousand seven hundred and eighty nine.

VOID WHERE PROHIBITED BY LAW

THE Conventions of a number of the States having, at the time of their adopting the Constitution, expressed a desire, in order to prevent misconstruction or abuse of its powers, that further declaratory and restrictive clauses should [illegible]d: And as extending the ground of public confidence in the Government, will best insure the beneficent ends of its institution:

RESOLVED, by the SENATE and HOUSE of REP[illegible] [illegible]NITED STATES of AMERICA in Congress assembled, two thirds of both Houses concurring. That the following Articles be pro[illegible] Le[illegible] se[illegible] [illegible]tates, as Amendments to the Constitution of the United States; all, or any of which articles, when ratified by three fo[illegible] [illegible] [illegible]all [illegible] and purposes, as part of the said Constitution, viz.

ARTICLES [illegible] U[illegible]tates of America, proposed by Congress, and ratified by the Legislatures of the several States, pursuant [illegible]

Article the first ...... After the first enumeration req[illegible] [illegible] Representative for every thirty thousand, until the number shall amount to one hun[illegible] [illegible]ss, that there shall be not less than one hundred Representatives, nor less than on[illegible] [illegible]umber of Representatives shall amount to two hundred, after which, the proportio[illegible] [illegible] less than two hundred Representa[illegible] nor more than one Representative for every fi[illegible] [illegible] [IN[illegible]

Article the second .... No law, varying the compensation for [illegible] Representatives, shall take effect, [illegible] electio[illegible] [illegible]tatives shall have intervened. [Not Ratified]

Article the third .... Congress shall make no law respecting [illegible]lishment of religion, or prohibiting [illegible] [illegible]ridging the freedom of speech, or of the press; or the right of the people peaceably to assemble, and to peti[illegible] [illegible]ss of grievances.

Article the fourth ..... A well regulated Militia, being necessary to the security of a fre[illegible] [illegible] to keep and bear Arms, shall not be infringed.

Article the fifth .... No Soldier shall, in time of peace, be quartered in any [illegible] owner, nor in time of war, but in a manner to be prescribed by law.

Article the sixth ...... The right of the people to be secure [illegible] their person[illegible] papers, and effects, against unreasona[illegible]rches and seizures, shall not be violated, and no Warra[illegible] upon proba[illegible]le cause, supported by oath or affirma[illegible] [illegible]larly describing the place to be searched, a[illegible] [illegible]eized.

Article the seventh ... No pe[illegible] [illegible] for a capital, or otherwise infa[illegible]rime, unle[illegible] [illegible]ctment of a grand jury, except in cases [illegible] in the land or Naval forces, or in the Militia, when i[illegible] service [illegible]ger; nor shall any person be subject [illegible] the same offence to be twice put i[illegible]pardy of life or [illegible] shall be [illegible] case, to be a witness against himself, nor be deprived of life, liberty, or p[illegible] without due pr[illegible] nor s[illegible] taken for public use without just compensation.

Article the eighth ..... In all criminal prosecutions, the accused shall [illegible] the right to a [illegible]ublic tri[illegible] of the State and district wherein the crime shall have been committed, which dis[illegible] [illegible]all have been [illegible]scertaine[illegible] [illegible]formed of the nature and cause of the accusation; to be confronted with the wit[illegible] against him; [illegible]lsory pr[illegible] obt[illegible] [illegible]itnesses in his favor, and to have the assistance of counsel for his defence.

Article the ninth ...... In suits at common law, where the value in contro[illegible] shall exceed [illegible] be right [illegible] by jury shall be preserved, and no fact, tried by a jury, shall be otherwise re-examined in a[illegible] [illegible]rt of the Un[illegible]tates [illegible]ccording to the rules of the common law.

Article the tenth ...... Excessive bail shall not be required, nor excessive [illegible] nor [illegible] and unusual punishments inflicted.

Article the eleventh .. The enumeration in the Constitution, of certain rights [illegible]onstrued to deny or disparage others retained by the people.

Article the twelfth .... The powers not delegated to the United States by the [illegible]titution, nor prohibited by it to the States, are reserved to the States respectively, or to the people.

Frederick Augustus Muhlenberg Speaker of the House of Representatives.

John Adams, Vice-President of the United States, and President of the Senate.

ATTEST,

John Beckley, Clerk of the House of Representatives.

Sam. A. Otis Secretary of the Senate.

DISTRIBUTED BY SOCIETY FOR INDIVIDUAL LIBERTY 304 EMPIRE BLDG, PHILADELPHIA PA 19107 - $1

NO MORE! A Gallery of Protests and Demonstrations

Bill of Rights: Void Where Prohibited by Law poster
distributed by the Society for Individual Liberty, c. 1969.
Yanker Poster Collection, Prints and Photographs Division,
LC-USZC4-1549

707 782 9000 WWW.POMEGRANATE.COM

Pomegranate

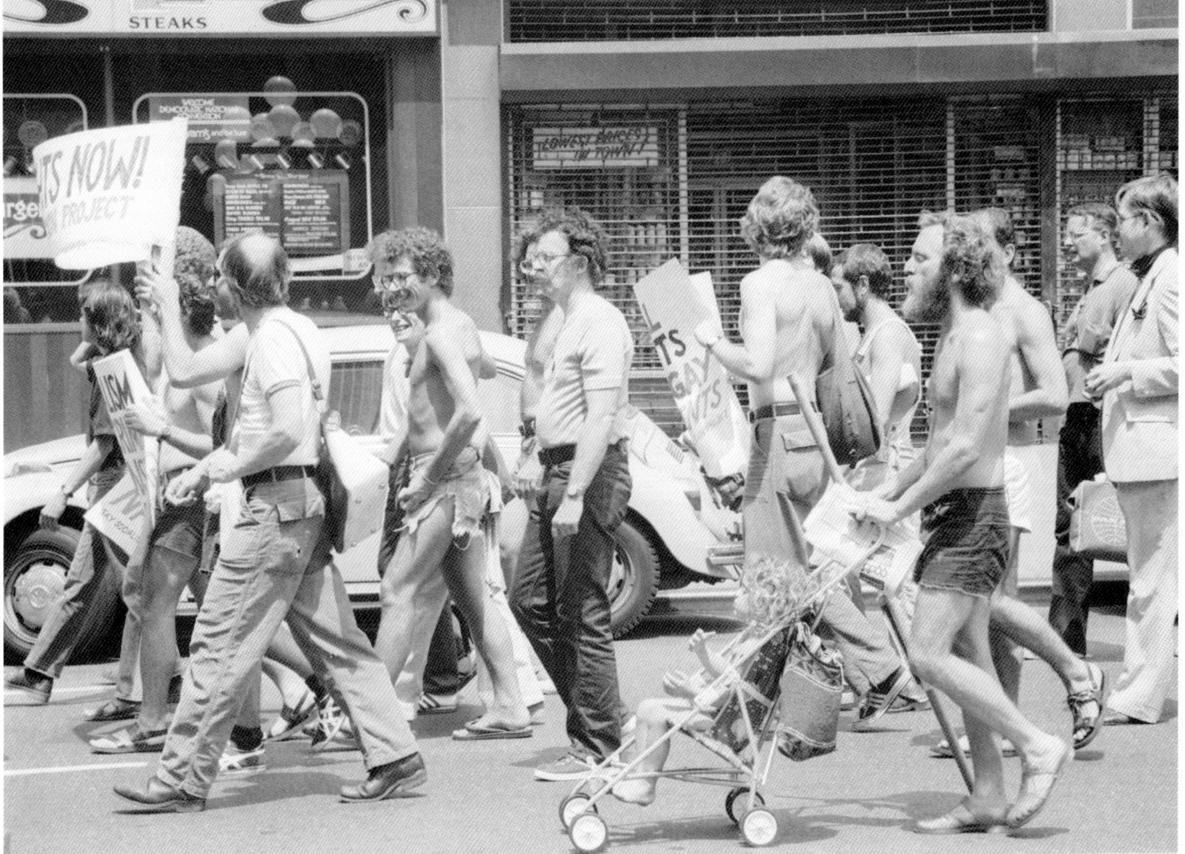
STEAKS
LOWEST PRICES IN TOWN!
TS NOW!
PROJECT

NO MORE! A Gallery of Protests and Demonstrations

Participants in the gay rights demonstration during the Democratic National Convention, New York City, July 11, 1976. Photograph by Warren K. Leffler. US News & World Report Collection, Prints and Photographs Division, LC-U9-32917-36

Pomegranate 707 782 9000 WWW.POMEGRANATE.COM

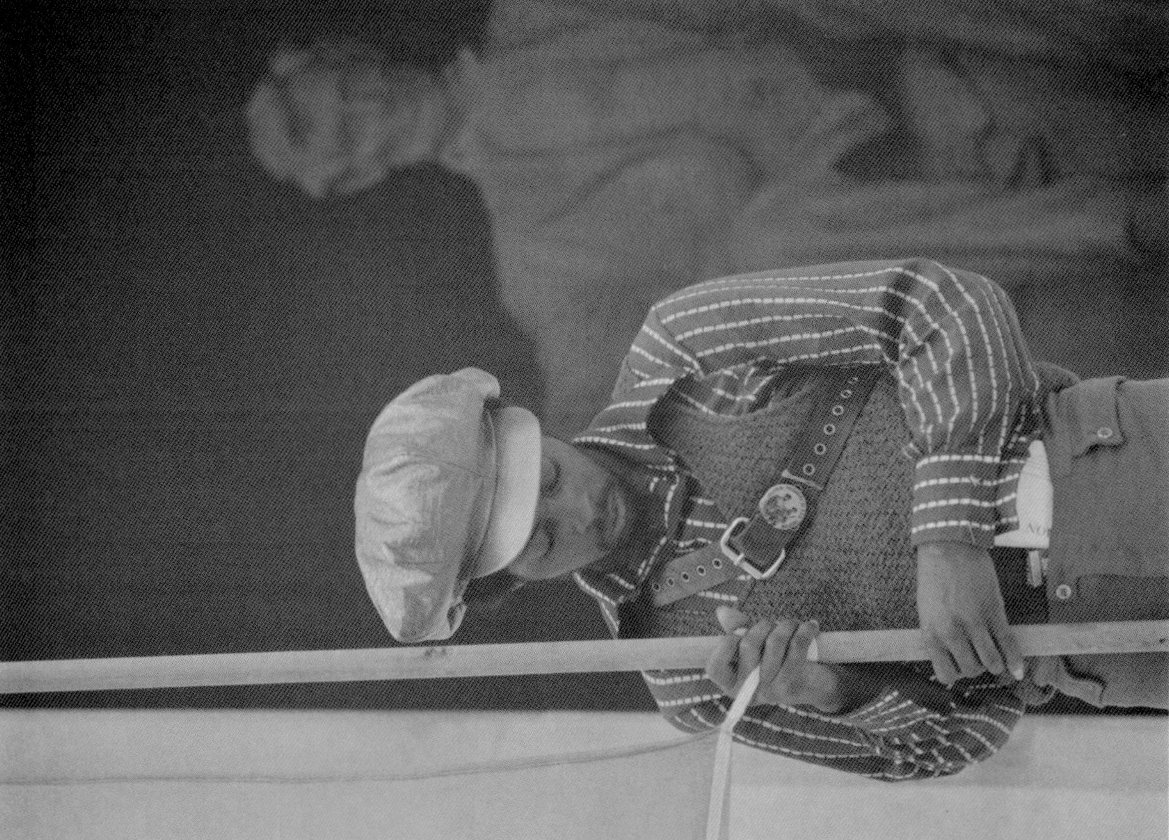

NO MORE! A Gallery of Protests and Demonstrations

On the steps of the Lincoln Memorial, a Black Panther holds a banner for the Revolutionary People's Constitutional Convention, Washington, DC, June 1970. Photograph by Warren K. Leffler or Thomas J. O'Halloran. US News & World Report Collection, Prints and Photographs Division, LC-U9-22860-6

Pomegranate 707 782 9000 WWW.POMEGRANATE.COM

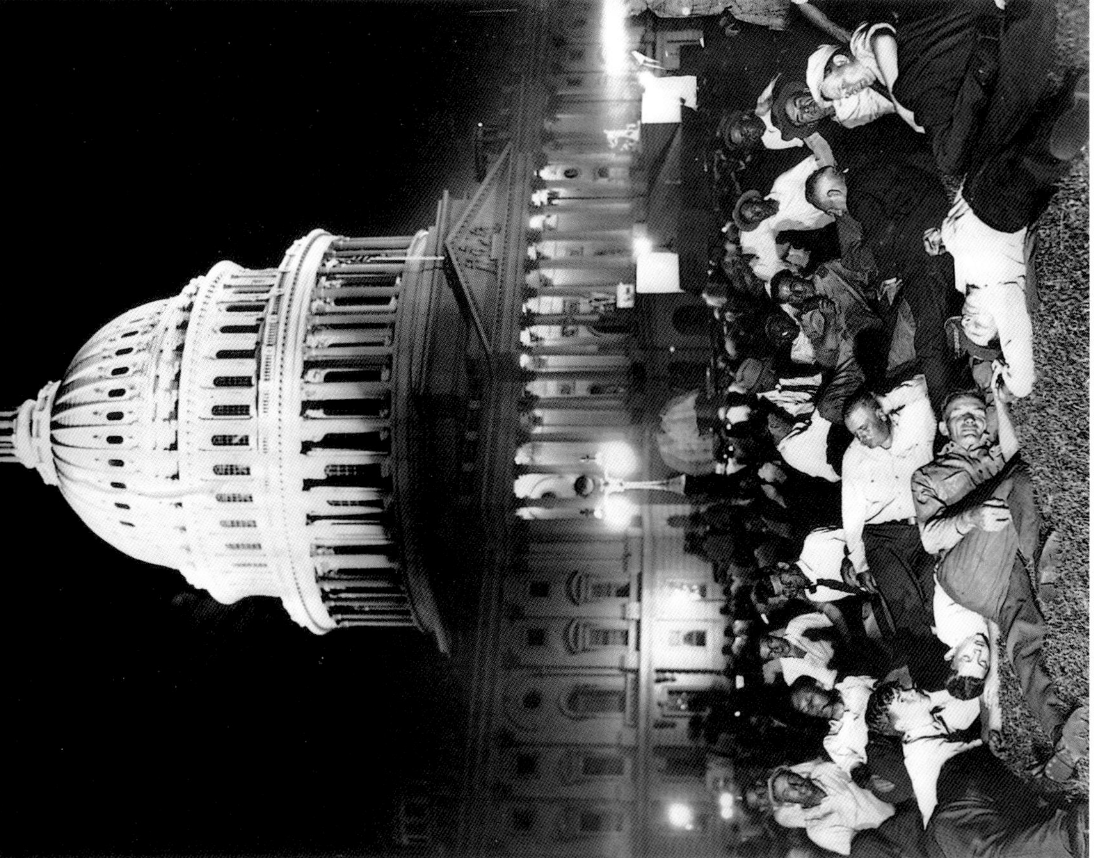

NO MORE! **A Gallery of Protests and Demonstrations**

Seeking the extra compensation promised them for their service in World War I, Bonus Army members camp out on the Capitol lawn, Washington, DC, July 1932. Photograph by Underwood & Underwood. Prints and Photographs Division, LC-USZ6-525

707 782 9000 WWW.POMEGRANATE.COM

Pomegranate

PICKET
LADIES TAILORS
STRIKERS
PICKET
LADIES TAILORS
STRIKERS

NO MORE! A Gallery of Protests and Demonstrations

Women tailors on a picket line, New York City, February 1910. News service photograph. George Grantham Bain Collection, Prints and Photographs Division, LC-DIG-ggbain-04507

707 782 9000 WWW.POMEGRANATE.COM

Pomegranate

CIVIL LIBERTIES
IN WAR TIMES
By Max Lerner
CITY WIDE FORUM
ROOSEVELT HIGH
JAN. 24TH – 8 P.M.
IOWA ART PROGRAM WPA

NO MORE! **A Gallery of Protests and Demonstrations**

"Civil Liberties in War Times," a lecture by Maxwell Lerner, American educator, author, and syndicated columnist, Des Moines, IA, January 24, 1940. Silkscreen poster, Iowa Art Program. WPA Poster Collection, Prints and Photographs Division, LC-USZC2-866

707 782 9000 WWW.POMEGRANATE.COM

NO MORE! **A Gallery of Protests and Demonstrations**

Students locked inside Sproul Hall at the University of California, Berkeley, following a daylong sit-in protesting rules restricting campus political activity, 1964. New York World-Telegram & Sun Collection, Prints and Photographs Division, LC-USZ62-121446

707 782 9000 WWW.POMEGRANATE.COM

Pomegranate

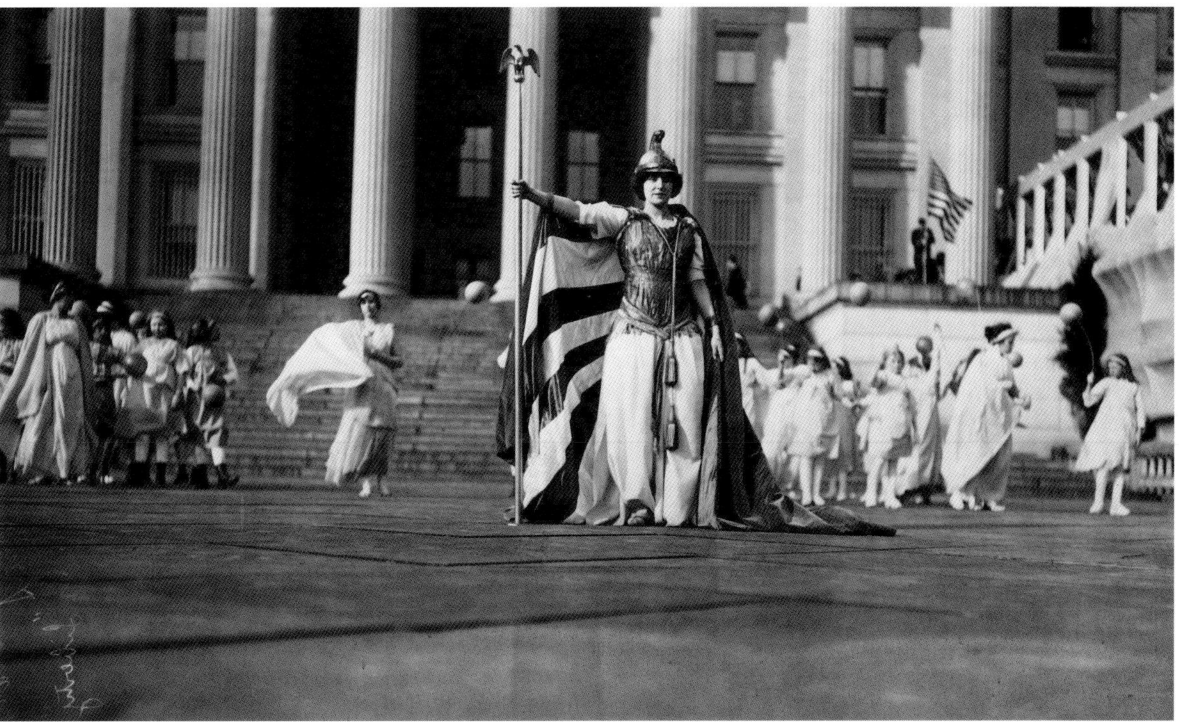

NO MORE! A Gallery of Protests and Demonstrations

Hedwig Reicher as "Columbia," and other participants at women's suffrage pageant at the Treasury Building, Washington, DC, March 3, 1913. News service photograph. George Grantham Bain Collection, Prints and Photographs Division, LC-USZ62-70382

707 782 9000 WWW.POMEGRANATE.COM

THE ISOLATIONIST
"AM I MY BROTHER'S KEEPER ?"
AMERICA WILL NEVER ACCEPT
THE CURSE OF CAIN!

NO MORE! A Gallery of Protests and Demonstrations

The Isolationist: Am I My Brother's Keeper? poster issued in support of the World Cooperation Campaign on the tenth anniversary of the outbreak of World War I. National Council for Prevention of War, Washington, DC, 1924. Prints and Photographs Division, LC-USZC4-767

Pomegranate 707 782 9000 WWW.POMEGRANATE.COM

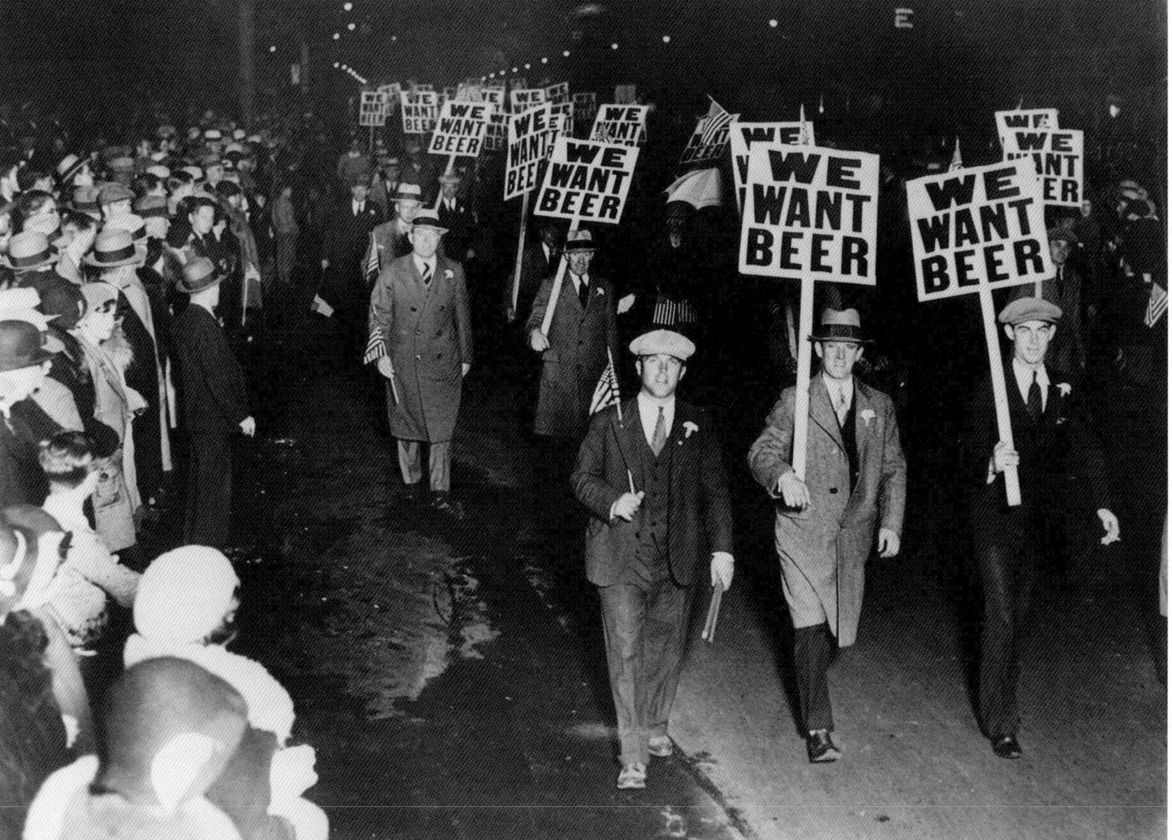
WE WANT BEER
WE WANT BEER
WE WANT BEER
WE WANT BEER
WE WANT BEER

NO MORE! A Gallery of Protests and Demonstrations

Anti-Prohibition labor union members march along Broad Street with a clear message, Newark, NJ, 1931. New York World-Telegram & Sun Collection, Prints and Photographs Division, LC-USZ62-123216

707 782 9000 WWW.POMEGRANATE.COM

OUR GRIEF IS NOT A CRY FOR WAR
N 40°44.120'
datamap_exit.art
W 073°59.452'
union.square 09/22/01_12:21:03
union.square>ground.0 – brg. 242° dist. 0.96mi.
union.square>exit.art – brg. 040° dist. 0.93mi.
exit.art>N 40°43.390' W073°59.920'
adhoc artist group +++ artists network of refuse & resist
www.artistsnetwork.org

NO MORE! A Gallery of Protests and Demonstrations

Artists display their messages at Union Square, New York City, in a performance responding to the terrorist attacks of September 11, 2001. Photograph by Jim Costanzo, "Reactions" exhibition by Exit Art / The First World, Inc. Prints and Photographs Division, LC-DIG-ppmsca-01701

707 782 9000 WWW.POMEGRANATE.COM

APPLE
TURKEY 60
65

NO MORE! **A Gallery of Protests and Demonstrations**

Civil rights activists seated at a lunch counter during a sit-in, Nashville, TN, 1960. New York World-Telegram & Sun Collection, Prints and Photographs Division, LC-USZ62-126236

707 782 9000 WWW.POMEGRANATE.COM

NO MORE! A Gallery of Protests and Demonstrations

Tens of thousands of demonstrators converge on the National Mall during the March on Washington for Jobs and Freedom, August 28, 1963. Photograph by Warren K. Leffler. US News & World Report Collection, Prints and Photographs Division, LC-U9-10363-5

Pomegranate 707 782 9000 WWW.POMEGRANATE.COM

OLD SOLDIERS NEVER DIE...
YOUNG ONES DO
©PRO-ARTS KENT, OHIO

NO MORE! **A Gallery of Protests and Demonstrations**

Old Soldiers Never Die: Young Ones Do poster by Pro Arts, Inc., Kent, OH, c. 1967. Yanker Poster Collection, Prints and Photographs Division, LC-USZC4-2877

Pomegranate
707 782 9000 WWW.POMEGRANATE.COM

MRS. P. LAWRENCE

JANE ADDAMS

ANNA MOLLOY

PEACE

PEACE DELEGATES ON NOORDAM

NO MORE! **A Gallery of Protests and Demonstrations**

World War I peace delegates, including Mrs. P. Lawrence, Jane Addams, and Anna Molloy, aboard the *Noordam* on their way to The Hague, April 1915. News service photograph. George Grantham Bain Collection, Prints and Photographs Division, LC-DIG-ggbain-18848

707 782 9000 WWW.POMEGRANATE.COM

Pomegranate

DEMOCRACY
and POLITICAL
PRISONERS
DON'T MIX.
SHALL
JUSTICE
DIE?
WE ARE
INNOCENT
VICTIMS.
WE ARE
WIVES
AND
CHILDREN
of POLITICAL
PRISONERS
4 YEARS
SINCE I SAW
MY DADDY.

NO MORE! **A Gallery of Protests and Demonstrations**

Children and women demonstrate in front of the White House, demanding the release of their fathers and husbands who were imprisoned during the war for violating the Espionage Act, 1922. National Photo Company Collection, Prints and Photographs Division, LC-USZ6-1820

Pomegranate 707 782 9000 WWW.POMEGRANATE.COM

REMEMBER
ATTICA

sept.13 7:30pm
attica memorial rally and service
mount morris park 120th st & 5th ave

NO MORE! A Gallery of Protests and Demonstrations

Remember Attica poster for a memorial rally following the 1971 prison riot in New York. Yanker Poster Collection, Prints and Photographs Division, LC-USZC4-2879

707 782 9000 WWW.POMEGRANATE.COM

E.A. DRINKARD GR
Coca-Cola

NO MORE! **A Gallery of Protests and Demonstrations**

Participants in the 1965 march from Selma to Montgomery, AL, which covered 54 miles, bringing attention to voting rights. Photograph by Peter Pettus. Prints and Photographs Division, LC-USZ62-133090

707 782 9000 WWW.POMEGRANATE.COM

LA DESTRUCTION DE LA STATUE ROYALE A NOUVELLE YORCK
Die Zerstorung der Koniglichen Bild
Saule zu Neu Yorck
La Destruction de la Statue royale
a Nouvelle Yorck

NO MORE! **A Gallery of Protests and Demonstrations**

The destruction of the statue of King George III in New York City on July 9, 1776. Hand-colored etching, printed Chez Basset, Paris, c. 1776. Prints and Photographs Division, LC-USZC4-1476

Pomegranate 707 782 9000 WWW.POMEGRANATE.COM

STRIKE PARADE 9/14/16
3989-7

NO MORE! **A Gallery of Protests and Demonstrations**

Streetcar strikers parade along the tracks, New York City, 1916. News service photograph. George Grantham Bain Collection, Prints and Photographs Division, LC-DIG-ggbain-22858

707 782 9000 WWW.POMEGRANATE.COM

MP

NO MORE! A Gallery of Protests and Demonstrations

En route to the Pentagon, protestors organized by the National Mobilization Committee to End the War in Vietnam clash with federal troops, October 21, 1967. Photograph by Warren K. Leffler. US News & World Report Collection, Prints and Photographs Division, LC-U9-18184-35

707 782 9000 WWW.POMEGRANATE.COM

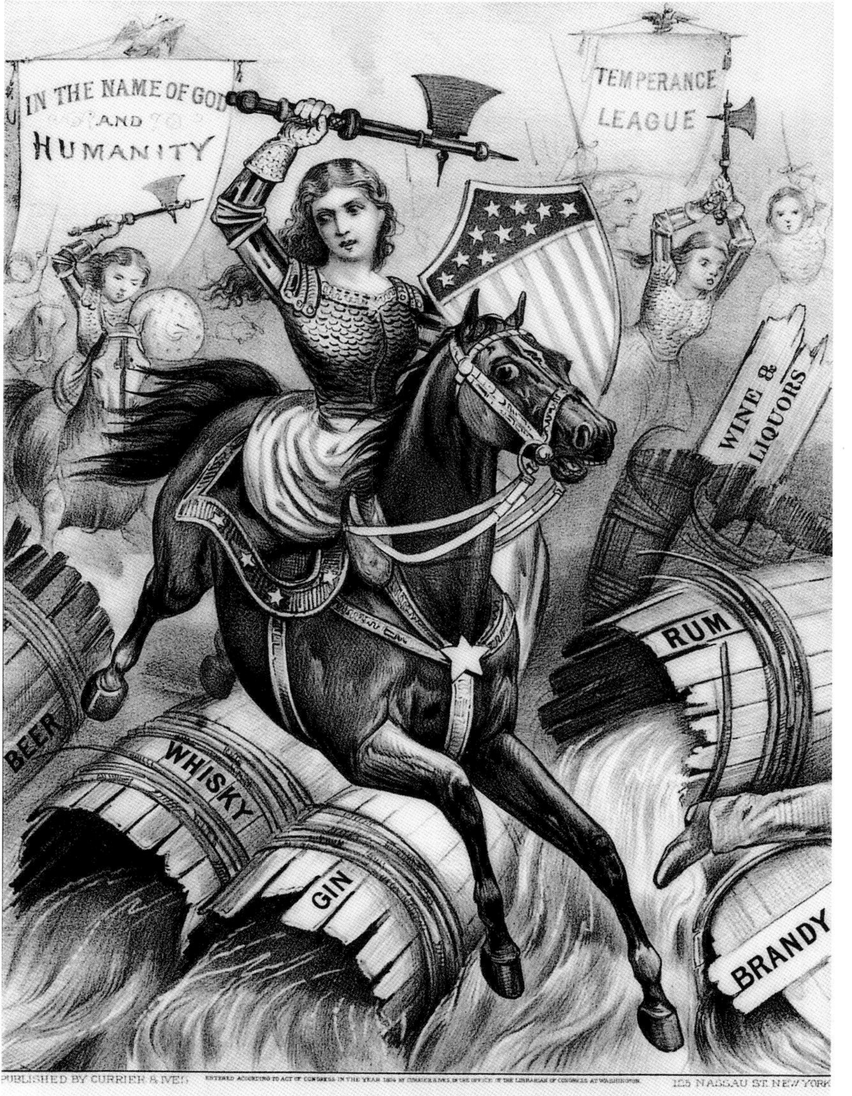
IN THE NAME OF GOD
AND
HUMANITY
TEMPERANCE
LEAGUE
WINE &
LIQUORS
RUM
BEER
WHISKY
GIN
BRANDY
PUBLISHED BY CURRIER & IVES
125 NASSAU ST. NEW YORK
WOMANS HOLY WAR.
Grand Charge on the Enemy's Works.

NO MORE! **A Gallery of Protests and Demonstrations**

Woman's Holy War. Grand Charge on the Enemy's Works, a print promoting the nineteenth-century crusade for temperance and prohibition. Lithograph, Currier & Ives, New York, c. 1874. Prints and Photographs Division, LC-USZ62-683

707 782 9000 WWW.POMEGRANATE.COM

Pomegranate

NO MORE! A Gallery of Protests and Demonstrations

Garment workers parading on May Day, New York City, 1916. News service photograph. George Grantham Bain Collection, Prints and Photographs Division, LC-USZ62-41871

Pomegranate

707 782 9000 WWW.POMEGRANATE.COM

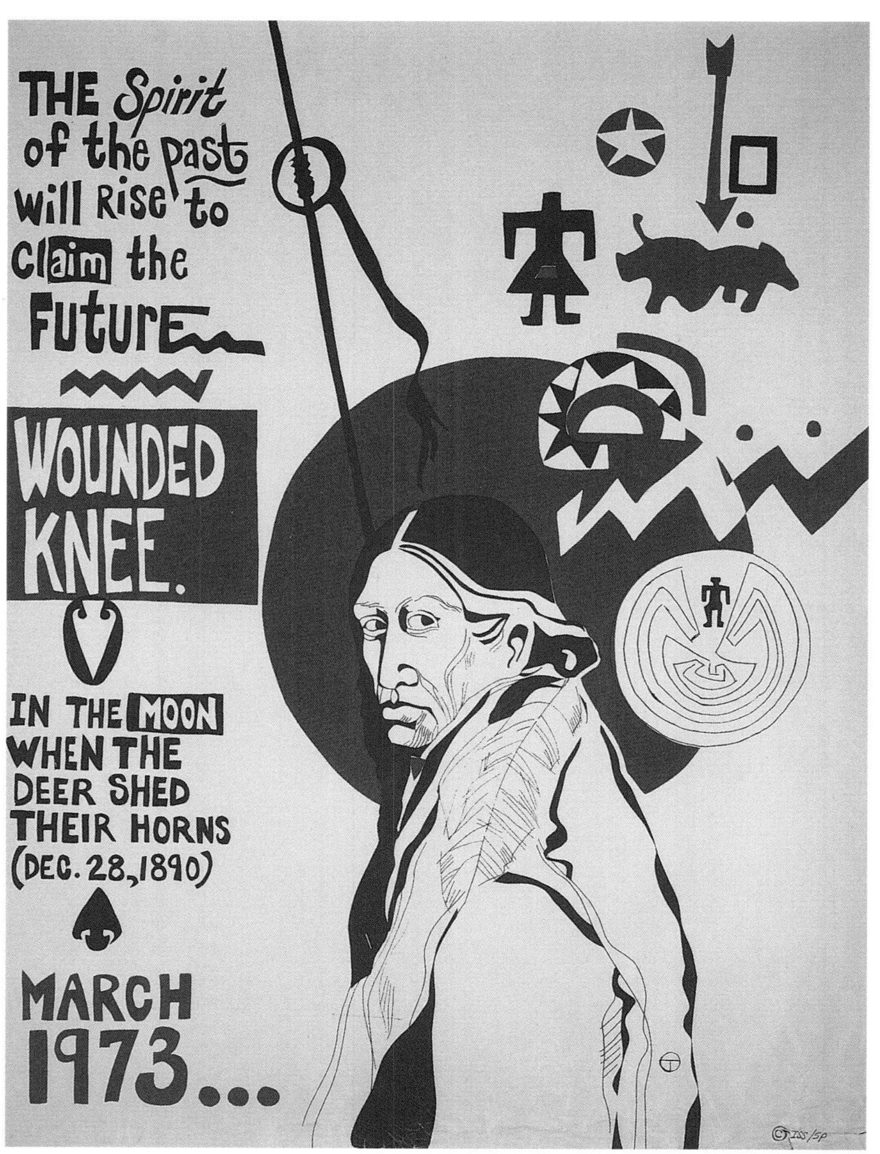
THE Spirit of the past will rise to claim the Future
WOUNDED KNEE.
IN THE MOON WHEN THE DEER SHED THEIR HORNS (DEC. 28, 1890)
MARCH 1973...
©ISS/SP

NO MORE! A Gallery of Protests and Demonstrations

The Spirit of the Past poster referring to the 1890 massacre and the 1973 siege at Wounded Knee on the Pine Ridge Indian Reservation, SD. Yanker Poster Collection, Prints and Photographs Division, LC-USZ62-126057

Pomegranate 707 782 9000 WWW.POMEGRANATE.COM